Primitive Pottery

Grass-fired pot, by author, approximately 24 inches in diameter.   Glazed circle from fused white lead.

Primitive Pottery

Hal Riegger

VAN NOSTRAND REINHOLD COMPANY
New York Cincinnati Toronto London Melbourne

I gratefully dedicate this book to my long-time friend,
Jack Lenor Larsen

Credits and acknowledgments

To the authors of *Papago Indian Pottery,* Fontana, Robinson,
Cormack and Leavitt, University of Washington Press, Seattle,
1962, for their permission to quote a pottery firing as done
by Listiana Francisco.

To Brad Johnson, for permission to publish his theme, "How
to Build a Fort."

I wish to especially thank my friends Peggy Dickinson and
Jack Leggett for their help with information and photographs,
Peggy on the Fiji Island potters and Jack on the Nigerian potters. My sincerest thanks also go to Gillian Hodge, who helped
me in many important ways.

The Firsk Potters are living examples of the philosophy behind this book; from them comes a faith in future attitudes.
I am happy.

Van Nostrand Reinhold Company Regional Offices:
New York Cincinnati Chicago Millbrae Dallas
Van Nostrand Reinhold Company International Offices:
London Toronto Melbourne

Copyright © 1972 by Litton Educational Publishing, Inc.
Library of Congress Catalog Card Number 75-184821

Line drawings by Carol Hannum
Designed by Rosa Delia Vasquez
Color printed by Princeton Polychrome Press
Type set by Modern Craftsmen Typographers

Published by Van Nostrand Reinhold Company
450 West 33rd Street, New York, N.Y. 10001
Published simultaneously in Canada by
Van Nostrand Reinhold Ltd.

1 3 5 7 9 11 13 15 16 14 12 10 8 6 4 2

Making A Fort

First you have to find a place to make a fort. Then you out-line it. After that you start digging till you get it deep enough. Then you put boards on and while there's still a little hole in the roof you make a fireplace. After that you make a door. Then you get in and seel off the cracks. Then you get out and get a bucket or something and fill it about to inches up with water and put dirt in it. After that you get some old news-papers and put them on the boards and put the mud over it and it is all finished. I guess.

(Theme written by Brad Johnson, age 10,
Gridley, California, 1967)

Preface

Some of my readers will wonder, "Why go backward in your craft and write about primitive ways of making pottery?"

Ceramics is one of the oldest crafts and its technology may not keep pace with that in other areas. But recently it has made significant advances for a craft that seems tenaciously to have hung onto the past— in maintaining centuries-old mechanical methods and being very slow to research and adapt new materials and methods. Many things are now taken for granted that did not exist sixty, or even fifteen, years ago. I think of two, for example: Pyrex glass and space capsule nose cones. Entertaining the thought of relinquishing these advances would be insane!

A few American Indians work in the primitive way, I suspect, like a few well-known Mexican potters, for the tourist trade. People in other parts of the world still work this way because they have not learned other methods, and their mode of living does not require a change. Some of us, like myself, do it even though our experience and knowledge have progressed much further.

For twelve years I have been working this way, for the most part, in preference to the more generally known ways. Why do I find primitive pottery interesting to the extent I do? And why do I feel it so pertinent to teaching?

Without explanation, I could reply, "I like to make pots this way," and there could be no challenge. Yet, while no defense is necessary, an explanation helps. Justification is found in the effect upon people as well as in the effect upon the resulting pots. In its simplicity and therefore its demands upon the skills of the potter (which are greater because of the technical simplicity) a manner of clear, logical thinking is brought about. We are, in a sense, taken back to the uncluttered thinking of children. Not only is this refreshing in so complex an existence, it is good training for the mental processes.

Contents

Perception: seeing design in desert junk.

Introduction

Throughout the world, wherever man found clay and discovered he could shape it with his hands and harden the resulting forms with fire, he experienced, in its most elemental and basic form, what we now call ceramics. Clay is a plastic mineral that can be permanently hardened in red heat.

Countless techniques and a vast store of knowledge have evolved from these two important facts about clay. No industralized country is without its society of professional ceramists who represent an economically important industry; hardly a person today is unaware of ceramics, and in North America universities offering ceramic courses number into the hundreds, let alone the thousands of elementary and secondary schools that also offer classes in pottery.

Yet ceramics can still be defined fundamentally as the craft and industry of forming objects out of plastic clay and firing these objects so as to harden them permanently. In this book on primitive ways of making pottery these fundamental, direct concepts must be remembered and practiced.

Footprint in fired clay. Origin not known, but probably New Mexico or Arizona.

Shard; basket-like coil construction. New Mexico.

"Primitive" is a difficult word to use here and needs some explanation. Archaeologists are not at all agreed on how to use the word. Perhaps we should dream up a new one.

In a discussion once of my pottery activities with a member of one of the southwest American Indian tribes, the word "primitive" was rejected in favor of "traditional" to describe them. Yet this is not correct either. But it does point out that primitive, as applied to art and to the craft or making of objects, in no way implies crudity. If anything, craftsmanship was on a higher level than we are apt to see nowadays. The materials were not refined or man-made and were taken from nature as they were found, wherever and whenever man chose to express himself through art. I have no doubt that man then observed the qualities and character of natural materials around him far more accurately than we do now, and used them quite sensitively and selectively for what they were and what they could do and convey. Hard and soft woods, feathers, bark, animal furs and hides, obsidian, jade, walrus whiskers, nacre—these were the materials nature provided, not to mention clay, the material of our concern in this book.

So I would like to look at it this way: "primitive" defines the way we will observe our materials (awareness) and the way we will go about using them (sensitivity) or, in other words, our approach towards pottery fashioned and fired in a primitive manner without the tools of modern technology.

Much early pottery around the world is similar, whether it was made in what is now England, or in Africa, the South Pacific or Japan. All of this was happening before these lands had their present identity. Apparently man's needs for existence and his intelligence were pretty much the same the world over at this stage of his development. Of course this did not all happen at one time, some areas in the world saw the first development of the craft of pottery while in others it came later. In some places (Africa, southwestern United States, and Fiji, for example) people are still working in a primitive fashion; in some places this occurs alongside of the most advanced technology we know.

Imagine man, any early man, as he stepped onto some soft clay, feeling its slipperiness, its ooziness (a good feeling), and later perhaps noticing that his footprints remained in the clay as it dried out. Lesson number one, and a very elementary one: clay can be formed and it will retain its shape.

When or how the jump was made from the footprint to the realization that clay could line a woven basket and make it more "grain-proof" is not known. We are even making an assumption when we suppose the first fired clay pots were derived in this fashion, from the lining of baskets which (presumably) got near enough to a camp fire to burn and leave a fired shell of clay.

Supporting the basket theory, aside from those shards indicating that clay was indeed pressed onto some woven object, is the fact that early pottery surface decoration or enrichment was directly taken from the patterns left by woven grasses and fibers. Such texture was made often with the fingertips or with a stick; interestingly it proved to be an excellent manipulation of the clay to join the ropes or coils from which early pots were made.

The approach to pottery I make in this book is as though experiencing it through the eyes and mind of early man. There was observation first, perhaps exploration followed, and it was not until many, many centuries had passed that man accumulated enough experience to project ahead to establish a goal in his mind and then engage in a series of experiments that would reach that goal. Let us assume in this book that we are not that far advanced.

Personally I very much like doing pottery in a primitive fashion, but when I write about it I wish to call attention clearly to the fundamentals of ceramics.

Dried clay, washed by rain into large depression. Death Valley, California.

1.

Earth Minerals

Solid bank of clay. Zabriskie Point, Death Valley, California.

In my book on raku* I discussed the use of commercially prepared clays of different types and also wrote of finding clays in nature: what to look for and briefly how to tell their characteristics. I was, and still am, interested in using local clays wherever I can, and while this is appropriate to raku it is essential in the context of this book.

Clays are to be found widely scattered over the face of the earth; in each of the United States clay can be found. True, clays are not all alike, and potters and industry do not by any means use all of them—industry because they have not the desired characteristics or occur in quantities too small for commercial use; potters through ignorance or because they hold a preconceived idea about what clay should be, in addition, of course, to the fact that a certain clay may really not be suitable for their established program. This kind of thinking is out of place here. I still maintain that any clay is good provided one is willing to learn how to use it (and it is only fair to say "good" includes, in some cases, the use of clay only as a slip coating or a glaze).

This attitude then places a responsibility upon the potter. He will have to do some experimenting, be observant, and draw conclusions, he is, in reality, starting off as a primitive potter!

What do you look for and need to know about clay? First, its property of plasticity: variable, certainly, but consistent enough by comparison to other minerals to be considered one of the prime attributes of clay. I think it is easy enough to determine if plasticity exists in the wet material and certainly one can wet a dry material to see if it is slippery or sticky, and therefore more or less plastic.

*Raku, Art & Technique, Van Nostrand Reinhold Company, 1970.

16

Where a deposit of material has dried, leaving deep cracks throughout its surface, it is indication of a degree of plasticity. Such cracking will be seen only in open, flat areas where the material has collected with water, has remained in a depression, and become dry.

In addition, noticing erosion where there are hills and banks will help locate material of some plasticity. Clays do not erode as much, or as quickly, as other mineral and organic soil, and therefore stand out. Rocks are an exception.

Next, color; but since we are not trying to find a clay with certain predetermined characteristics, this will be of no importance here. But it is helpful to realize that almost invariably the color of raw, wet or dry clay is different after it is fired. In the raw state one will look for mustard, gray-green, dark brown, terracotta reds and gray.

Third, the potter will now have to discover how his clay handles; how easily can he work it into plastic condition; how does it handle in building; what methods of construction are best for a given clay; what kind of timing must he observe during construction (can the pots be formed quickly, or must the process be slow); how does the clay dry; is there a tendency for the clay to crack in drying? All these questions are answered by observation and will tell the person much about the clay he is using.

Very simply, there are the two broad types of clay I have experienced that are important to know about: First, the truly plastic clay that tends to be slippery and, in workable condition, bends from one position to another easily without cracking. Second, the seemingly plastic clay that is sticky and builds easily, but will not bend too well; it must be put into position when soft and more or less left there; it will hold in horizontal position better than true plastic clay. It is a far less pure clay, sometimes with considerable acid organic material in it, and could generally be classified as silt. But it works, it fires beautifully, and if one can cope with it through the drying stages all is well. This second type of clay is very different from that which we are used to. For example, it will build easily and dry up to the point of leather hardness, then suddenly it seems to curl up its toes, crack all over, and warp considerably.

Soft clay. Death Valley, California.

If, at this stage, the work is dried very slowly, pieces will come through successfully. This kind of clay can accommodate a considerable amount of filler. Fillers (non-plastic minerals) are sand, volcanic ash, grog, or any finely divided material that is mixed with clay in amounts up to 50 per cent. The exact amount will have to be determined with each specific clay.

It is physically possible to use refined clays purchased from suppliers, but this will defeat an essential quality so desirable in primitive pottery. Far better that, for total character of the work, and for experience in this particular field of pottery, one find clay somewhere in the field. Commercially produced clays are usually too highly refined to fire successfully and must be altered considerably before they will even work. By contrast, many unrefined found clays are technically far superior for the kind of firing they will get.

Photographs accompanying this chapter show more or less what to look for in clay. There are not any hard and fast rules. Trial mixtures are made and their working and drying properties noted. If change is indicated because of failure then adjustment is made; but this should only be based on the demands of physical properties of the clay and never because of a lack in personal working adjustments to its nature.

I believe this discussion illustrates one of the definitions of "primitive" in that it points out how a process may be simple. It also points out how sensitive and adept the craftsman must be.

Dung-fired pot, by author, approximately 16 inches in diameter.

Wood-fired pot, by author, approximately 20 inches in diameter.

2.

Shards showing fine and coarse temper.
New Mexico and Arizona.

Preparation of Earth Minerals

Highly plastic or dense, compact clays are not satisfactory to use in making things to be fired primitively. Some kind of aggregate, either of small or large particle size, must be used with them. The reasons are twofold.

One concerns drying the clay after a piece is made. Drying conditions in the field are much less controllable, and therefore not as satisfactory, as those in the shop. Sometimes pieces will dry quickly, as on hot, dry days, while at other times they will dry slowly. Usually the drying tends to be uneven, and more attention must be given to pieces than when they dry in the shop. This situation can be eased by preparing a clay mixture that dries easily and at the same time reduces warping and shrinking. This is common knowledge to potters, who often practice adding a non-plastic mineral to their clay.

The second reason will be discussed more fully later because it concerns the reaction of dry clay pots to the rapidly rising temperature of the firing.

What we today call non-plastic filler is referred to by anthropologists as temper, in clays Indians used. Since the Indians were scattered all over the United States, and peoples of other countries extended the geographical range around the world, it is reasonable to assume there were many different kinds of temper used in clay mixtures. In the southwest United States, temper is often mica or a form of volcanic ash.

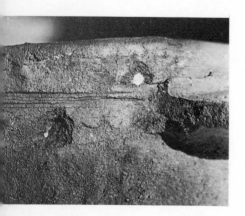

Limestone pop-outs in fired clay. Limestone particles in clay or temper may not be identified until after firing. They should be avoided for the reason shown in this picture.

Other tempers used in the past include sand, micaceous clays, and finely decomposed rock.

All of these tempers serve the purpose for which they were intended, although mica and volcanic ash are best, because their chemical composition resists heat shock. However, in the context of working primitively with pottery, various tempers should be considered more or less satisfactory. The choice is based on the material's availability, its particle size and quality, and its fired color.

It seems important to me that particular attention be given to particle size. The addition of coarse or fine temper to clay affects the mix differently. Fine temper will maintain a smooth character to the clay while "opening" it; coarse particles will naturally make a rougher clay. It should be remembered that when identical amounts are added, fine temper will reduce plasticity in a clay and absorb more water than will coarse temper.

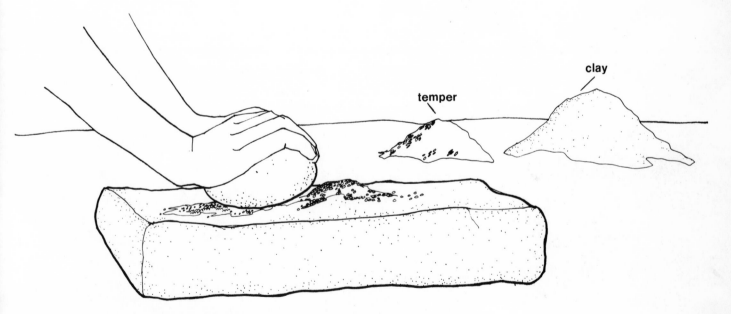

Grinding temper. Highly valued by Indians as tools that improve with use, two stones grind temper that often is found as decayed, chunky rock.

Kneading (wedging) clay.

The condition of clays found in the field will vary. Sometimes they are wet; provided the potter does not wish to refine such a clay he can proceed to wedge, or knead, his temper into the clay, if temper is needed. Sometimes the clay is dry and may be so hard it needs grinding. In most cases proportions will be approximate. They are determined and measured, the ingredients are blended thoroughly, and, if dry, are placed into a bucket in alternate layers with water and allowed to soften. Subsequently the mixture is worked up into a thoroughly consistent mix.

Proportions of temper, or filler, and clay will vary depending upon the several factors mentioned earlier. As a general rule to follow, temper is used in amounts of from about 10 per cent up to as high as 50 per cent.

Potters who mix their own clay will age it several days, or up to several months or longer. The Sung Dynasty Chinese potters prepared clay for the next generation. Aging is not necessary and is not usually possible in the field. The southwest American Indians never aged their clay and used it immediately after preparing it; in fact they did not prepare clay until they were ready to make pots. If this seems odd it will help to remember that forming is done by hand and not on the potter's wheel. The requirements of the clay are different.

Sifting clay and temper into water.

Screening clay in preparation for making a wet mixture.

25

3.

Tools of the Fiji Island potters: paddles,
stones, and gourd for water.
(Photo by Peggy Dickinson)

Tools

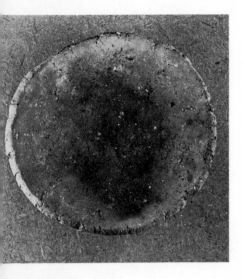

Fired clay puki.

The subject of tools can be dealt with briefly.

Not because there were only a few tools used in making pottery; there were many. It is only that a description of them and their use is superfluous. Tools in the past were found objects that helped the potter to do certain things better as he was building or decorating his pot. Included were such objects as shells, portions of gourds, sticks, smooth, hard stones, and chewed yucca leaves—used for scraping, smoothing, attaching coils of clay, polishing, and painting decorations onto the clay surface.

It would be unfortunate if a person felt he had to collect all manner of manufactured pottery tools and take them along on a primitive pottery-making excursion. Far better that he look around to find what objects he can use for certain specific operations. This helps achieve in the work a character not found in pottery elsewhere and made differently.

The accompanying photographs illustrate a puki and some of the found objects I have used as tools.

Found tools for pottery making: shell, twig, polishing stone, rock, and pieces of wood.

Implements used in shaping pottery.

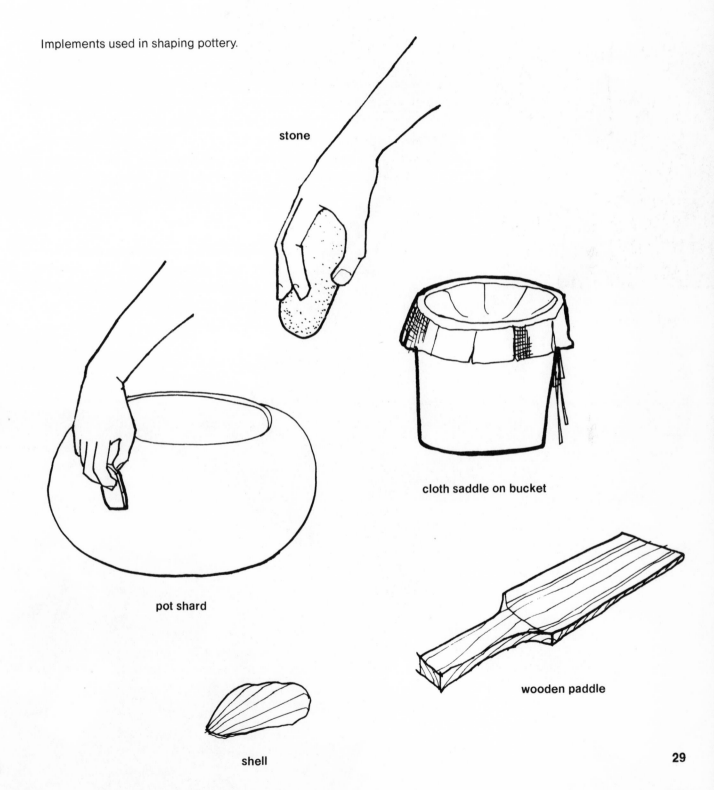

stone

cloth saddle on bucket

pot shard

wooden paddle

shell

4.

Ten minutes after starting the pot: beating from the inside with wooden pestle while turning the pot with the feet and hand. Note puki underneath. Garki, Kano, Nigeria. (Photo by Jack Leggett)

Forming

Making pottery in the studio calls on various techniques of forming clay that are known as throwing, casting, and hand-building. In this book we are concerned only with hand-building.

This category, unfortunately, becomes fragmented in people's minds to mean slab construction, the pinch-pot method, coil-building, and the like. I do not necessarily frown on separating the various techniques of hand-building since it helps define and clarify the activity for many people. But I do feel that it should be separated into its various categories in a different way, one that does not have the inhibiting effect I have so often noticed. Hand-building should be thought of in terms of how the hands manipulate clay naturally, and with consideration for its consistency.

Most of us are so accustomed to working with clay in its usual plastic condition we forget it exists in several other states: fluid, soft paste, leather-hard, and dry. In reality it is only when we are aware of clay in its various states or conditions that we can use it to full advantage. It will soon be discovered that one may use clay in several consistencies when making a pot.

It is helpful if clay is thought of as being manipulated by the hands or a tool. What are the natural motions made by a person the first time clay is in his hands? He squeezes, pats, bangs, or pinches it, and he twists and pokes it and rolls it into a ball or coil. When he is shown how to join clay together properly, he will then have at his command all the normally required techniques for hand-building pottery. One manipulation of clay often overlooked is taking clay away from clay, which is also known as carving or scraping with a sharp tool, or gouging with the fingers. Some clays encountered in the field will not respond successfully to any other treatment.

Joining clay strip to partly built pot. (Photo by Richard Simpson)

Thinning strip by pinching clay upward. (Photo by Richard Simpson)

Parging (smoothing) inside of partly built pot. Women's pottery, Ilorin Tribe, Yoruba, Nigeria. (Photo by Jack Leggett)

Japanese potters are especially sensitive to the physical characteristics of the clays they use as well as to the need to work with it in the right consistency and with the correct methods. Two examples illustrate this. Acid jars produced in one Japanese province are cast with clay slip in two separate pieces, which are joined together at the proper time; later a neck is thrown on the top. Huge bowls are thrown in sections on the potter's wheel by successively adding coils to the rim, throwing them to extend the size, and drying the clay somewhat each time. This is continued as far as necessary. The method is the only way possible to make a large bowl on the wheel with this particular clay.

Another aspect of clay-working worth remembering is how the element of time enters and how it is used advantageously. Because of the combination of form and clay character, the construction of some pots will necessarily extend over a longer period of time than was anticipated. People are often seen struggling with a sagging pot, propping it up with crumpled newspapers or some such thing, or stuffing its interior with rags. How absurd! What an admission of lack of skill, lack of observation or sensitivity! Why not build the pot more slowly, letting each clay addition stiffen a bit before adding more?

But using time well does not always mean waiting. When making pottery by primitive methods the potter often will be working in the sun, or at least in a warm, dry climate. Here the reverse is true: he better get on with his work or all will be lost. The potter must develop a constant awareness of time that is so much a part of his work that he is not usually conscious of it.

The conditions under which the pot dries should influence both the form and construction of the work. If the reader has ever made any relatively flat objects, such as plates, tiles, or shallow bowls, he will have noticed there are problems in drying them. Invariably he has had to fight to keep the edges from drying and cracking, while the centers remain damp. Under the most ideal conditions these are difficult forms to dry. Easy to make, yes, but not easy to dry, and particularly to fire by the methods discussed later in this book. My own experience shows that most flat shapes are inappropriate to primitive firing. When one looks back upon the objects made by early potters one rarely, if ever, sees flat forms. We know that early pots were influenced by such natural forms as gourds, fruits, and squash, yet I have no doubt the demands of firing were also responsible.

Potters are thus cautioned against expecting much success with flat, slab forms in the firing. Brief reference here to the primitive methods of firing pottery will help explain why. Although we will deal later with very rudimentary kilns, primitive firing essentially implies the firing of pottery without kilns. The enclosure that contains, and helps control, heat in more sophisticated kiln firing is lacking, and it may be imagined that even distribution of heat around the ware is difficult if not impossible. The uneven heat distribution results in uneven expansion of clay during the firing, which creates stresses the clay cannot withstand. By contrast to the success obtained in kiln firings, even the highly skilled southwest American Indians today lose pieces through firing. Once chosen as the way of permanently hardening pottery in the fire, the primitive method has to be accepted for what it is; other aspects of the work must bow to its demands.

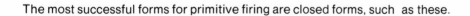

The most successful forms for primitive firing are closed forms, such as these.

Clay pieces can be built on the ground, which, if dry, is an excellent support while working; a hole can be made to conform to the shape wanted on the bottom of the piece. This is not to say the earth is used as a mold, although it might be. The American Indians in Arizona and New Mexico, and early potters elsewhere, used a puki, a previously made and fired clay saucer on which they built their pieces. Fired pots can also be used to support and shape new pots. Recently I noticed plastic store-bought bowls used for this purpose. Potters in the San Ildefonso and Santa Clara areas of New Mexico can be seen using pukis today and, I might add, having used them myself for over twelve years, I find they serve as an excellent equivalent to the plaster batt used in the potter's studio. In Oaxaca, Mexico, potter Donna Rosa can still be seen using not one, but two pukis, back to back, in building her pots. She literally throws the neck onto a hand-built pot, spinning the form with one hand while throwing with the other. Her two pukis used this way may indicate a step in the evolution of the potter's wheel.

Building a pot directly in an earth depression.

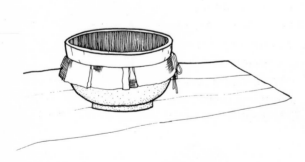

Plastic or clay bowls are also used today to form the bottom side of pots. A cloth separates the clay from the bowl, keeping it from sticking.

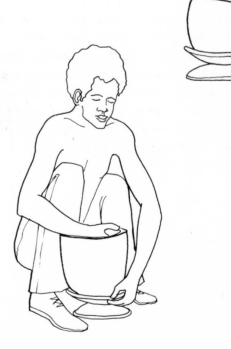

Handbuilding a pot on two pukis, back-to-back.

As long as pukis are small like those the Indians use, or not larger than about 5 inches in diameter and less than ½ inch thick, they can be fired in the field in a pit fire. If they are to be larger it is safer to make them in the studio and fire them ahead of time in a kiln.

I have noticed at least two techniques out of the past that have been handed down to primitive potters working today. One is where the paddle and anvil are used in shaping pots and thoroughly joining the sections of clay together. The paddle is literally a paddle shaped by the potter from wood, while the anvil is a smooth rounded stone, asymmetrical, with surfaces that fit a variety of curves. The other is the practice of completing the rim of a pot first, a technique still being done by many potters. A ball of clay is punched with the fist into a thick, rounded, shallow bowl and the rim size established. It is thinned to the proper thickness and allowed to stiffen somewhat. Then the belly of the bowl is extended and given its proper form with the paddle and anvil. No joints have been made in this piece, so the paddle and anvil serve an additional use by compressing the clay to make a stronger pot.

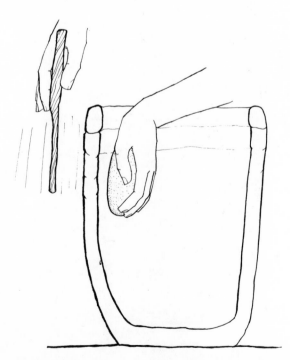

Paddling the pot walls with a stick and stone shapes it and makes good joints.

Building large urn over old fired pot; pounding with a rock. (Women's pottery, Ilorin Tribe, Yoruba, Nigeria. (Photo by Jack Leggett)

Author starting a pot on a puki and joining the first strip. (Photo by Richard Simpson)

Correct use of a puki; the pot curves upwards before reaching puki's edge. (Pot by Jim Lewis)

Incorrect use of puki; clay came out over edge but fortunately resulted in a good-looking pot. (Pot by Ruth Culbertson)

The Fiji Island potters hand-build pottery in a way rarely, if ever, seen elsewhere. The nature of their clay apparently demands this complicated procedure.

For tools they use a cutting tool, stone, and paddle and a reed-formed base on which to work that is used in the same way as a puki.

The steps in making the pot are as follows: One of three balls of clay is beaten with a stone into a thick, small bowl and is laid into the puki; the other two balls are patted by the hands into oval pancakes. With the stone, paddle, and fingers, one slab is joined to the small bowl; the second is then joined to these when the piece is paddled and scraped into form. A disc is cut from the side and used to close the top. The pot is dried a bit and turned upside down; what was the bottom is now the top and the clay is damper here. Another disc is cut from this top and used to close the side hole. A strip of clay is added to the top, then shaped and smoothed with the paddle and stone to finish the pot. The piece is then dried in the normal way.

Fiji Island women making pottery. (Photos by Peggy Dickinson)

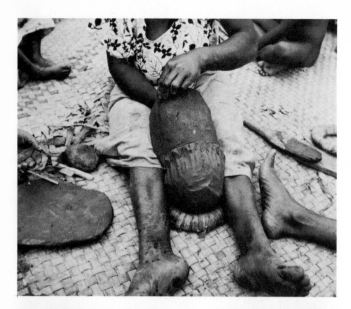

Fiji Island women making pottery.
(Photos by Peggy Dickinson)

5

Incised drawing done with a stick. Fort Walton culture, Florida

Surface Enrichment

Decoration of primitive pottery is intimately related to the tools mentioned earlier. Technically it is simple, and aesthetically it should be simply conceived. The fire will inevitably lend its effect to the clay surface, usually in ways not precisely controlled by the potter; thus, this somewhat unplanned result must always be in his mind as a possibility when, and if, he chooses to decorate the pot's surface. It is happy, then, that the tools are simple and the methods elementary.

Traditionally, no glaze is involved. The clay surface, its texture and color are what are considered. Surface enrichment can result from the manner of building a pot, such as with coils, or overlapping leaves of clay not totally smoothed on the outside, and revealing some evidence of joints. A paddle used for refining the form will also leave its marks, especially if it is rough.

Texture resulting from scraping wet clay bowl with a serrated tool. Bowl of black fippleware from Qaw el-Kebir, Middle Egypt, approximately 3 inches high. (Photo, courtesy of the Trustees of the British Museum)

Overall texture resulting from the fingers joining coils. (Pot by author)

Patterns, textures, units of design can be placed upon, or into, the clay surface in addition to what develops through shaping. The Nigerian potters roll a length of rope over the soft clay surface of their pots, leaving a pattern not unlike that of woven baskets. Sticks can be used to draw into the soft clay surface. Indians of the early Fort Walton culture in Florida created particularly interesting designs on their pots this way. Other Indians have developed patterns of a more refined nature, more precise and smaller in scale, with what must have been a very sharp tool.

Thick, wet string rolled onto pot's surface makes this texture. Garki, Kano Province, Nigeria. (Photo by Jack Leggett)

Delicate, incised line drawing. Shard from New Mexico.

Incised border. Bronze Age cinerary urn. Cornwall, Great Britain.
(Photo, courtesy of the Trustees of the British Museum)

Modeled animals on rim of bowl. Matmar, Middle Egypt, Predynastic
(Negadi I) Period. (Photo, courtesy of the Trustees of the British
Museum)

The primitive pottery of the Amratin period of Great Britain is only one example of applied modeling. One of the best examples of modeling is again from the Fort Walton culture and shows formed knobs or handles on pots. These people were all sensitive to the fragile character of clay pots fired at low temperatures. To my knowledge such appendages as the present-day handles on pitchers were never attempted, and whatever handles the old potters needed on pots were either very small or were slight protuberances. Usually they were placed within a protecting curve in the pot and made pots easy to lift.

Modeled handle on rim of bowl. Shard from Fort Walton culture, Florida.

Protected, slightly recessed handle on pot made by author.

Decorative clay strip paddled onto pot's surface. (Pot by Betty Feves)

Southwest American Indians are well known for their painted decoration. A yucca leaf chewed at one end to remove the pith is their brush. Earth colors, such as ochres, white burning clays, as well as syrups made from the sap of desert plants and trees are painted on the pot with it. Black is obtained by applying these organic syrups and baking them to less than red-heat. Like other fired colors, it does not wash off. Reds, blacks, and whites are painted into religion- and mythology-inspired patterns in the angular form of basket decorations.

Painted decoration suggesting basket weave, done with earth color. Shard from New Mexico.

Decoration painted with earth color. Shard from New Mexico.

Cooking mesquite sap and water to make a liquor for painting designs in black on the pot. Mesquite and locust sap are used in other parts of the world for decorating and waterproofing pottery. The two trees are related.

Turtle with painted ochre decoration. Santo Domingo Pueblo, New Mexico. (By Robert Tenorio)

Sketchily polished clay on shard.
Hohokam Indians, Arizona.

Among the most sensitive and humorous designs on pots are, to my way of thinking, those done many hundreds of years ago by the Mogollon potters in what is known as the Mimbres style. Animals are delightful, moving about in often humorous ways on the pot's surface. These decorations show great skill with tools.

New Mexico potter Maria Martinez and her husband Julian are well known for their San Ildefonso black pottery on which decoration appears as a matte pattern on a shiny surface. On a highly polished clay surface are painted designs with a thin solution of clay and water, the effect of which is to destroy the polish. This draws attention to yet another way of treating the pot's surface.

Polishing with a very hard and smooth stone is done on the leatherhard pot. Indian potters treasure a polishing stone. Maria Martinez and some other potters of the southwest polish the entire surface of their pots. Donna Rosa in Mexico uses the polishing stone in what I feel is a more creative fashion. Her polishing *is* decoration, born of the shape of the pot and the natural movement of her forearm. Her beautiful curved designs always seem to be in close harmony with the pot's form. How could they be otherwise? While Maria's patterns are matte finish, Donna Rosa's are glossy and are obtained in a different manner, yet both use the same tool. Still other present-day American Indian potters combine polishing with raised or carved designs.

Primitive fired pot; its beauty lies not in decoration, but form and
the few bits of gravel picked up by wet clay. (Pot by Rick Dillingham)

Drying pots around a small fire. (Photo by Richard Simpson)

6.

Drying

The pot is now finished and a concept has been fulfilled; nothing more can be done with it save what a capricious fire can do. The pot is complete. My emphasis is intentional.

Although potters do not project in the mind beyond a dry pot to the glaze as often as they should, there are those who do conceive a pot through to the final firing, including the use of glaze. Here, however, there is no glaze to be used, and consequently no thought is given to its color, preparation, or application. Except when using organic syrups for decoration, the potter making pieces by the primitive methods must realize that all he intends to do to the pot is done before its only firing.

From the wet or leather-hard stage a pot will be dried slowly or quickly, depending upon its size, thickness, and the clay of which it is made. Small or thin pieces can be dried much faster than large or thick ones; clays that are more open (containing more non-plastic material) can be dried more quickly than fine, dense clays.

Dry pot by author ready for firing. Minimal decoration will not compete with fire-created colors. (Photo by Richard Simpson)

However one chooses to do this physically, it is still a good practice to dry the pot as evenly as possible. It may be dried upside down, or a paper or cloth put over its mouth to retard drying of the rim. Closed, hollow pieces, and especially those with small mouths, should be dried longer, as they do not give up internal moisture as easily and quickly as open pieces. They will often take twice as long to dry.

"Dry" is a word not usually understood accurately. It means absence of moisture. Absence of moisture is not a variable condition, but a very specific one. When damp clay is heated quickly to 212° F. or higher, any moisture will, with violent expansion, turn to steam. It is easy to imagine what happens. I feel this can hardly be emphasized too much, for I have seen too many pieces that were apparently dry blow up. Air drying is not always sufficient; it is doubtful there is any place on earth where air is absolutely dry. It cannot, alone, be expected to evaporate all the moisture from a damp pot. In many instances supplementary heat must be applied to complete the drying. One way to do this is by placing the pieces around a small fire and rotating them every so often to expose all sides to the heat. Drying is completed when the pot changes color and darkens.

Turning pots around while they are drying. (Photo by Richard Simpson)

Drying may take only an hour or it might take all day if the pots and fire are not given sufficient attention. There is no danger that a pot will be too dry for primitive firing!

This advice is not meant to contradict a different, relatively new practice among some potters, namely "wet" firing. This has no place, as far as I know, in the tradition or history of primitive firing, yet the circumstances of primitive firing are appropriate to wet-firing pots.

I do not know when the practice first started in this country. In an attempt once to explain to a novice how important it was that pieces be dry for the bisque firing, I shaped two small bowls and dried one completely while keeping the other wet. As I placed them both in the hot coals of a wood fire, I explained that what she saw would answer her question; I was more amazed than she was to watch both bowls fire in perfect safety! Her expression said, "So, what are you trying to tell me?" That was in 1965.

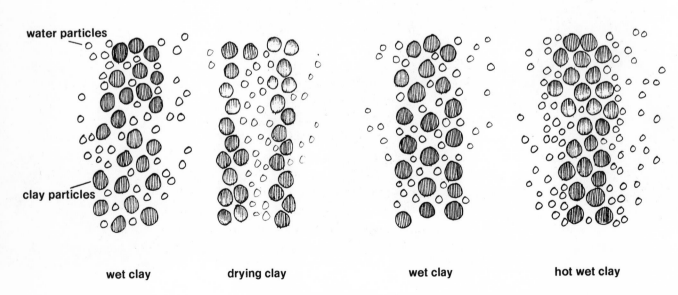

AIR-DRYING SITUATION   **WET-FIRING SITUATION**

water particles

clay particles

wet clay   drying clay   wet clay   hot wet clay

Cross-section drawings of the walls of pots, illustrating the theories of dry- and wet-firing.

Potters about the country who have been doing wet firing have experimented with glass and other inorganic fibers mixed into the clay along with considerable filler, making bodies that come through the wet firing admirably. There are various theories I have read about the phenomenon, but I present my own here, which is different.

If the potter has reached an understanding of the mechanics of wet firing he has reached an important understanding about clay particles and water.

Imagine at the start clay in workable condition. It is made up of variously sized particles with water surrounding them and filling tiny gaps in between. This water takes space. The particles do not all touch each other, but are separated by a film of water, no matter how infinitesimal it might be. Plastic clays are composed of smaller particles than are short clays and, when in workable condition, contain more water. During drying, this water leaves the pot, from the outside surface first, clay particles come closer together until they begin touching one another. Spaces between surface particles diminish, accounting for the familiar shrinkage of clay. But the inside of the pot's walls, the core of the clay, has not dried yet. Its moisture must still move outward to the surface to evaporate, but the spaces through which it must pass are now much smaller and consequently evaporation is much slower. This would be the way to visualize a normal air-drying.

Wet-firing places the pot suddenly into a temperature that may be as high as 1,600° F. There is sudden activity within the walls of the pot as they heat through quickly. As moisture is leaving the clay surface, moisture is also moving from the clay's core outward. This all happens so fast (maybe within a three- to five-minute period) that the clay actually dries from its core outwards, or just the reverse of what happens in air-drying. Thus, wet pieces can be successfully fired without blowing up, but cracks can appear in the walls or the pot slump into a heap. Adjusting the clay mixture will reduce, if not eliminate, these effects. I personally regard wet firing as fun, and I occasionally do it myself. But I believe there must be considerably more research done in this area before the results will justify the method of firing.

7.

Pot glazed with desert alkali and clay. (Pot by Robert Brady)

Simple Glazes

Glazes in the sense we know them today were not used on primitive pottery, yet certain techniques were used that approached the effect of glazes in that vessels were, to a degree, rendered watertight. For example, polishing the clay with a rock compacts the surface of the pot; the effect after firing is to slow the seeping of water or other liquids through this more dense surface layer.

Roman pottery, while not primitive in our sense, is noted for the use of "terra sigillata" (meaning "earth seal"). By means of the phenomenon of deflocculation, or the addition of a small amount of alkali to a thin clay slip, coarse particles were settled out, leaving on top a watery mixture containing only the finest of the clay particles. Terra sigillata was used to coat the pots and was applied, I presume, at the leather-hard state. Although its effect was similar to that of polished clay it was achieved in a totally different way. Provided a certain variety of clays is available, the advantages of terra sigillata over polishing are the range of colors and fine brush work possible.

In the context of a true glaze (a mixture of materials which, when fired to proper temperature, will form a glassy coating on the surface of vessels) we can indeed achieve glazes on primitively made pottery. Certain alkaline salts such as those of soda and potash, along with borax, are to be found in limited areas in the western United States. If he is fortunate to be near a dry lake or alkali deposit the potter can make a simple glaze with materials direct from nature. Many times I have been able to do this, and at other times and places have purchased plain borax from a grocery store. These fluxes can be combined with the same clay from which the pots are being made, in roughly equal proportions; I have varied the proportions all the way from 3 to 1 to 1 to 3, and all have been successful.* This should be interpreted to mean they fuse more or less. It is hardly worth being terribly scientific about this, since usually the clay composition is not known and, besides, primitive firing is far from accurate even if one has worked years with the same clays, the same fuels, in the same location, and under the same weather conditions.

I would certainly encourage the use of glaze so long as it is not conceived in the same way as when used in studio firing. Personally, I tend to regard its use as a decorative element.

One must be quite aware of what is happening to the pots during firing: they are on the ground and in direct contact with wood, grass, or dung and with the resulting ash from burned fuel. Any molten glaze on the outside surfaces of pieces is bound to hold this ash, or any grit or soil that happens to get into the fire. Whatever results is not to be considered bad or wrong, but as a natural outcome of working this way. To obtain a relatively smooth glazed surface, it is obvious that such areas must be protected from contact with fuel and ash, which is quite possible without exceeding the natural, logical limits of the total process. One way is described on page 70.

If glaze is applied only to the inside of a pot, it will be protected if the pot is fired upside down. Another way to protect glazed surfaces is to cover them with a piece of metal before placing fuel over the setting. Other solutions will come to the reader's mind as he gains experience with primitive firing.

A clay slip containing borax, or even a thin wash of borax dissolved in water, can be used decoratively. Whether these materials and their use could be called glazes and glazing is dubious, but it seems to me an honest method suited to the occasion. In a technical sense it could be likened to decorating techniques of the Greek Red and Black Ware. Manipulation of the firing can produce varied results, as will be discussed later.

Decoration of oxide and borax.
(Pot by Betty Feves)

*Recipes and molecular formulas (assuming clay content to be kaolin):

1. Borax   75 parts   (recipe)
    Kaolin   25 parts
              100

    $1\ Na_2O$ $2\ B_2O_3$ $.96\ SiO_2$ (molecular formula)
            $.48\ Al_2O_3$

2. Borax   25 parts   (recipe)
    Kaolin   75 parts
              100

    $1\ Na_2O$ $2\ B_2O_3$ $8.8\ SiO_2$ (molecular formula)
            $4.4\ Al_2O_3$

8.

A large setting of medium-sized pots enclosed with large logs to contain heat.

Firing Without Kilns

Firing pottery without a kiln is a simple and direct operation that brings the potter into intimate contact with his pots and the elements of firing in a way other, more sophisticated firings cannot. But, as with all simple processes not assisted by technical aids, considerable skill and experience are necessary for good results. Every part of the operation is the direct responsibility of the individual doing it. Because the process is simple does not mean its execution is without demands.

For the first time some rarely considered aspects of fire become important: heat rises, small pieces of fuel burn faster and hotter than large pieces, wind can make the heat of a fire lopsided. These and other things must be known and brought under control for successful firing.

Following the same train of thought, one realizes that the pots must be so placed that heat will entirely surround them, that there should be no sudden rise in temperature, and that the heat around the pots must be as even as possible. Pots are not placed in a pit and a fire built over them. Fuel is selected and used in a way that brings the temperature up gradually, and firings are avoided on windy days if possible.

Let us examine first the manner of setting the pots for firing. American Indians originally put their raw pieces on rocks. Out of experience they chose rocks that would not explode in the firing. If we do not know already, we must test rocks in a fire before using them.

The accompanying illustration shows how the Nigerian potters make a bed of twigs and branches upon which their pots are put; the effect is the same as with rocks in that heat will reach the bottoms of the ware as well as the sides and top.

Pot supported on three stones for firing.

Preparing for a firing. Bed of twigs on which pots are put. Pots at rear left are filled with burning grass to remove all traces of moisture. Garki, Kano Province, Nigeria. (Photo by Jack Leggett)

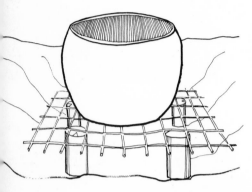

A pot supported on iron grating and tin cans for firing.

Potters also raise their pots off the ground with an old metal grating, or any old metal that can stand the heat. Later I will mention how this distance between earth and pots affects reduction and oxidation in firing (see Chapter 9).

It is apparent that pots can be fired at almost any location. The potter will first survey the surroundings to determine what objects are at his disposal, then proceed to set up for firing on that basis.

The second element of firing concerns fuel and how it is controlled. The potter will naturally choose a location providing more or less natural, and freely available, fuel, and such a site will likely be outside an urban area.

Placing a grid on which to fire pots.

Oil and gas, which need supplementary equipment, are not considered and have no place in this kind of firing; instead, fuels like wood, grass, coal, lignite, leaves, and animal dung are used. It matters not so much which of these is available so long as the potter knows how to use them.

Both the type of fuel and its form will affect the way the pottery setting is made. These two factors must be logically related to each other. Photographs show a variety of fuels used in firing.

Knowing how fuels burn is helpful: heavy, large chunks of wood burn more slowly than finely split wood; green wood burns more slowly than well-seasoned wood; dry grass burns faster and hotter than wood, but for a shorter time. American Indians in the past have used coal, lignite, and animal dung as well as wood, and are always sure to gather sufficient fuel before starting the fire. The Nigerians must amass great stacks of fuel because it is mostly grasses tied into bundles. It is far better to have gathered more than enough fuel than to have to scrounge frantically during firing.

The fuels about which I can speak with some authority are wood, grass, cow dung, and rubber tires. Wood is the most common, yet I prefer it the least. Both dung and grass are easier to handle, and with them I can avoid a too-sudden heat rise in the beginning. Of all the fuels I prefer dung; it catches fire easily and burns with a gentle, steadily increasing heat. Twigs or finely split wood are put under the pottery setting and lit, and dung is piled around and on top of the pots. Dung seems always to reach about the optimum temperature without getting too hot. Placed as it is, one or two layers thick around the pottery, it forms a protective barrier that holds in the heat during firing and keeps the pottery from cooling too rapidly after firing is completed. It is not necessary to slow the cooling by burying the pots and fire under dirt. This is true also of grass which, when burned, will leave a thick protective layer of fine ash all over the pots.

The fuels of primitive firing: dung, twigs, and wood.

Pots on a bed of twigs. Wood is next placed over them for the firing. Pot at right wrapped with wire to make a pattern during firing. (Pots by author)

A single, large pot being fired in dung. (Photo by Richard Simpson)

I quote here the schedule of firing as done by the late Listiana Francisco, a Papago Indian potter in Arizona:

At 5:00 A.M., the potter lights a small fire of palo verde wood in the bottom of her pit. (All potters fire their pottery in the early morning, when it is cooler.) She then returns the 200 or 300 feet to her house to eat breakfast. When breakfast is done, she goes back to her pit, arriving between 5:30 and 5:45. By this time the palo verde has burned down to a few hot coals and white ashes. The potter sets three fist-sized rocks down in the coals, places a sheet of tin on its side, and rests one large pot (such as a water jar or feast-size bean pot) on its side on the rocks. She then completes building the tin oven, roofing it over with a final piece of tin.

Next she places more palo verde sticks at the outside base of the oven where they promptly catch fire from the heat of the coals inside the oven. She adds numerous cakes of dried cow manure, finishing the fueling by tossing on—or more properly, setting on—sticks of mesquite.

The potter then waits until the fire has burned down to coals. Before she tears down the tin oven with a stick, the potter first removes the lid and checks to see if the pot inside looks fired. If it is not ready, she adds a few more mesquite sticks and fires it as long as necessary. If the pot seems to be ready, the potter knocks down as much of the tin oven as is necessary to be able to reach into the mouth of the pot with a stick and thus remove it by lifting the pot off its three-rock stand in the coals. She uses the stick to set the pot down on its side on three additional rocks laid there for that purpose about 12 feet or more from the fire. The pot is a rather dark gray, almost black color as it comes hot from the coals, but turns to a rich, light brown as it cools in the air. When the pot has cooled sufficiently to be handled, she gets it on the ground and wipes off the ashes and dirt with a cloth before taking it back to her house where it will be stored to await a buyer.

She then rebuilds her fire, this time placing two small su-guaro-sirup jars on rocks in the coals to be fired. By 8:00 A.M. these two jars have been fired, and she is through working on pottery for the day.

A single large pot fired in this manner requires about one and a half hours to be fired properly; the two small pots require thirty to forty-five minutes. The potter says that if the pot is a bluish color inside, then it is cooked completely and ready to be taken from the heat. After the pot has cooled, she tests it for serious fractures by striking it with her knuckles and listening to the ring. A clear ring indicates a well-made pot, with no cracks caused by firing.

From my own experiences with firing, I would avoid taking pots from the fire too soon. The accompanying photo shows the kind of experience I have encountered more than once by cooling the pot too fast; large pots are more inclined to crack than small pots. Perhaps Listiana Francisco was fortunate in having a source of clay and/or temper with good thermal shock properties. Many of us will not be so fortunate. If this was her situation, it would explain how she could remove hot fired pots so quickly from the ashes. It is also quite possible that I have fired my pots to a greater heat than she did. Very recently, in working along-side Elmer Gates, a Mojave Indian potter, I definitely noticed he fired to a lower temperature than I did. It is a well-known fact that clay fired to low temperatures will withstand heat shock far better than clay that is fired higher. Mrs. Francisco obviously had many years experience with a given set of materials and working conditions and knew well what she could do. My own experience will more parallel that of my readers, since I have worked with a variety of clays, tempers, and conditions and without a lifetime experience with any. A newcomer to primitive pottery firing is in unexplored territory and should therefore be prudent and not court disaster. Until the potter is experienced, I would recommend strongly that at the conclusion of firing the pots be completely buried under dry earth, and left to be dug up several hours later.

Pot taken from the fire too soon. Cooling too fast caused this severe crack.

When building the setting of pots for firing it is sensible to create a slight pit 6 to 10 inches below the ground level, and to surround it with a circular mound of loose, dry earth; then soil will be on hand when it is time to bury the fire. This kind of setting is often called a pit-firing, but should not be interpreted to mean firing in a deeply dug hole in the ground.

Next in importance is weather, and in particular the wind. You will have noticed that Mrs. Francisco did her firing early in the morning when it was cooler. But, also, at this time of day the chances are there will be little, if any, wind. Quiet air is a definite advantage to even firing. If one is not fortunate in having ideal firing conditions like this, some provision must be made to establish wind breaks on the windward side of the firing. Any object that performs this function is all right. Sometimes the wind is changeable, and a windbreak must be moved here and there around the fire. This can be difficult since it must be close to the fire to be effective, and is a nuisance to say the least. Sound advice is to fire only when the weather is calm.

Thus, having been briefed about what to expect with a firing, the potter gathers stones, old metal, or a bed of twigs to support the pots; fuel in sufficient amount to complete the firing; pieces of metal to form an "oven," or protection around the pots (helpful, but not a necessity).

Digging a shallow pit in preparation for pottery setting.

Establishing one proper way to fire a pot primitively.

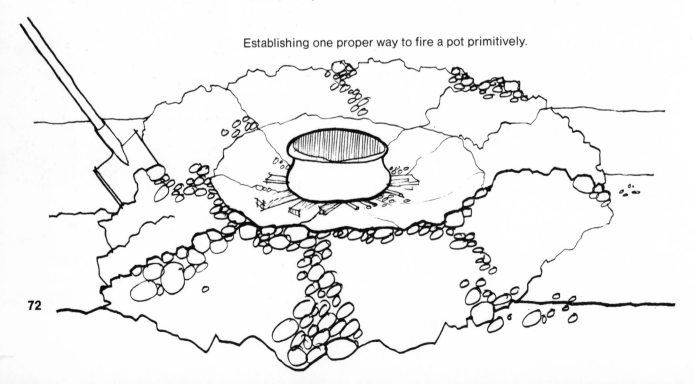

He next digs a shallow depression in the earth large enough for his pottery and the fuel, and he finally shovels a dam of earth around this. Preparation for firing will wisely follow Mrs. Francisco's, namely building a small fire first and letting it burn a while before putting the pots in place. This dries the earth and preheats pots placed around it. If the potter is not certain his pots are dry this is the time to make sure. Drying might take only a half-hour or it might be four or five hours, all depending upon: (1) how carefully the pots are attended and rotated, (2) how large or small the fire is and how consistently it is kept burning, (3) the size of the pots, (4) the density of the clay mixture, (5) whether the pots are open or closed forms, and (6) how close to the fire they are put. Regardless of the preceding, it must be remembered that there is no harm in over-drying any pot but that it can be disastrous to fire a pot containing any moisture whatever.

Firing setup as used by Mojave potter Elmer Gates. Here a true pit is dug about 3 to 4 feet deep. Chunks of mesquite wood overlaid with brush are underneath half of an oil drum. Pottery is put inside, the drum covered, and long sticks of mesquite put over and around the drum. This firing lasts about one hour, after which the pots are removed with a hooked rod. Very soon after this the remaining heat is used to bake the black decoration.

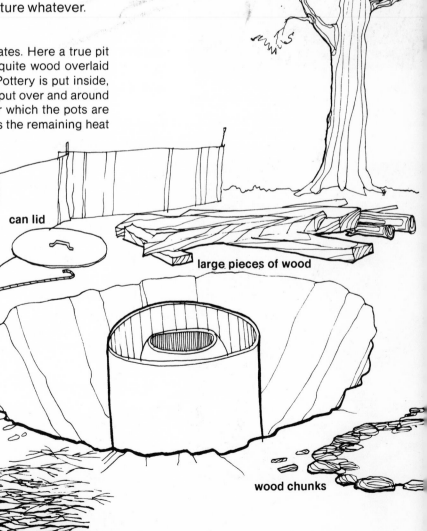

wind screen

can lid

large pieces of wood

lifter

brush

wood chunks

Metal is placed on supporting stones, over twigs, and single pot placed upside-down on it. (Photo by Richard Simpson)

Putting cow dung in place over the pot. (Photo by Richard Simpson)

Enough dung is put over the pot to complete the firing. (Photo by Richard Simpson)

When the potter is ready, the actual firing proceeds more or less as did Mrs. Francisco's. Different fuels will alter the physical aspects of the placement of pots and fire. With the exception of grass, enough fuel can be put over the pots in the beginning to complete the firing. It may not be easy to judge this the first time, but after three or four firings the potter knows how much is needed.

After firing with dung several times I have discovered that a single layer of the dung cakes is enough to fire pots properly, while more than this will sometimes overfire them. The fuel must be placed around and over the pots quickly and carefully within two or three minutes' time.

After watching a number of people make disastrous errors I would caution potters to be especially gentle with fuel of any weight or bulk; fragile pots are underneath and somehow, it seems, when they are out of sight this is forgotten! For this reason, and because when the fire is well under way it is too hot to add more fuel gently, it is wise to place all the necessary fuel on the fire at the beginning.

The approximate duration of the firing has already been mentioned. More specifically, small pieces up to 6 inches in size can be fired in less than an hour. Pieces up to 12 and 15 inches should take about twice as long, and larger pots even longer. However, lengthening the firing time beyond a certain point becomes meaningless. Firing here is understood to mean the time it takes to raise the heat to somewhere between 1,400°F. and 1,600°F., or clear red heat. It is not advisable for the fire to get hotter, and once this temperature is attained the firing is not continued. This point is stressed because so many potters are used to longer kiln firings they cannot believe primitive firing is done so quickly.

Using old spring car seats to protect pot from direct contact with burning dung.

A large number of pots being set into place for firing with scrap, green wood. Settings like this are fired more slowly to allow heat to penetrate to their centers.

A huge pile of pots being fired with grass. Women's pottery, Ilorin Tribe, Yoruba, Nigeria. (Photo by Jack Leggett)

Heavy pieces of wood placed gently around pottery.

Piling enough wood on a small pottery setting to complete the firing.

Two hours should be long enough for firing any pot or group of pots not larger than 3 feet in diameter. It is more difficult to fire these larger pots or settings evenly. When we see some of the huge jars made by the Tuzigoot Indians of Arizona, the considerable skill these people exercised in firing their work is appreciated. Some of their pots are easily 4 feet in their largest dimension.

If you are a stoneware potter you should compare the above description to what you are used to in your studio: nursing big pots or sculptures in the kiln overnight with only pilot flames on in the kiln, taking the kiln up ever so slowly to red heat, and so on. These things are well worth thinking about.

Tuzigoot pots. Two hand-built storage jars, black with fire spots. These huge jars measuring 3 to 4 feet attest to the skill in firing achieved by the Tuzigoot Indians of Arizona. (Photo: National Park Service)

One contemporary version of primitive firing with no kiln uses automobile tires that provide a concentrated and easily handled source of fuel. Whether one's ethics allow the use of tires is another matter, for they do give off a thick black smoke.

Setting rubber tires in place around pots for firing.

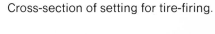

Cross-section of setting for tire-firing.

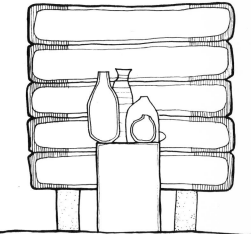

Right: A variety of colors obtained through primitive firing.

Below: Pot by author. Stick figures, units of design applied on surface. (Photo by A. L. Thompson)

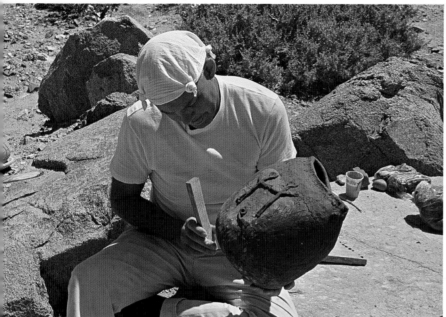

Pots drying around a fire.

Above, left: Windbreak used during dung-firing.

Above right: Raku kiln built of clay and sand; derived from design of kiln #5.

Kiln #1 in operation.

The same considerations are given to firing preparations for tires as were described earlier for other fuels. Physical dimensions of the tires dictate the size and number of pots that can be fired at one time. After the pots have been thoroughly dried, bricks, stones, cans, or a grate are arranged over the coals to support the pots within the inside diameter of the tires. Pieces are put in, then three, four, or five bricks or stones are placed in a circle around the setting to support the tires. Air entering underneath provides for better combustion inside. Then three or four tires are placed on these supports, and within a few minutes they will be ignited by the remaining coals. A stack of tires like this actually forms a kind of kiln, or wall, protecting pots from the cooler outside air as well as containing the fire's heat. Rubber is such a concentrated fuel that it will be impossible to avoid reducing the pots although sometimes they will reoxidize when cooling.

The main bulk of the tires will burn out in about one-half to three-quarters of an hour, but remaining sulfurous embers remain quite hot at least an hour longer.

The idea of using strips of inner tube and blown out tires found along desert highways came to some of us during a workshop in southeastern California in 1964. One particularly observant student, quite aware of the necessity to use what the area provided, came back to camp one day with his truck full of torn tires and rubber scraps, along with a small amount of scarce wood.

I have worked many times since with rubber in different forms, in open fires as well as for simple kiln firing. When used to fire pottery in an enclosure such as a kiln, rubber will burn more efficiently, but not without some smoke. This leads me to mention that tire retreading shops around the country accumulate enormous masses of scrap rubber shavings similar in size to sawdust. Whereas its use may not have a legitimate place in firing primitively, it seems to me potters might do some experiments on how to fire their kilns with this fuel efficiently and smokelessly. The rubber is free. Tire retreading shops have no use for it and only take it to our overloaded dumps for disposal.

Steps showing the setting and firing of pottery with rubber tires. Pots were put on a can to bring them into the area of greatest heat. Fire was started with sticks on two sides of the tires. Note how tires are sitting on bricks. At the end, one more tire added to complete firing.

Fiji Island Pottery Firing Today

As I write, more information has come to me about firing pottery in a primitive way; what follows will seem to contradict some of what I have already written. I therefore include it as a separate addition to this chapter, rather than worked into the body of information about firing.

It has bearing on our way of thinking, and our philosophy, let us say, clearly showing how the mind must be kept open and warning us of the folly of creating tight rules about our work.

Peggy Dickinson, a friend and fellow-potter who has recently been to the Fiji Islands and had the privilege of observing and working with the island potters, all women, reported on their method of firing.

Their procedure in setting up the pottery for firing does not differ essentially from what I have already described: split bamboo laid on corrugated iron forms the floor upon which the pots are put, and over which bundles of grass, split bamboo, and palm fronds are laid. But from here on the firing differs from what I have described earlier.

The firing site is on a low bluff "exposed to a tradewind which blows in a predicted direction each morning during the dry season." Photographs show potters setting fire to the kiln on the leeward side. The fire burns on this side for a few minutes before the windward side is lighted. Later, when the kiln is at full heat the strong wind is seen to be still blowing. The fire burned about one-half to three-quarters of an hour. The potter added grass bundles on windward side several times."

Of course no "kiln" is involved. It is a figure of speech this potter used. However, I think the point is made that specific rules, or procedures, if they are established, must apply only to a specific set of circumstances. The Fiji Island potters fired their pots in a wind but obviously the pots were successfully and properly fired.

We are again reminded of the basic definition of ceramics, that pieces are made from an earthy material that can be formed, which will retain that form and which, when fired to red heat or more, will become permanently hardened. As long as this is achieved successfully, it matters not how it is done.

Steps in the setting and firing of pottery with grass and palm fronds.
Fiji Island potters. (Photos by Peggy Dickinson)

Removing hot pieces from fire and daubing pitch on surfaces to
make them watertight. Fiji Island potters. (Photos by Peggy Dickinson)

Oxidation and Reduction

Oxidation and reduction are two words used to denote a condition of the atmosphere surrounding pottery whether it is fired in kilns or, as in the case here, without kilns. A potter will speak of an oxidizing or reducing fire, or while firing the kiln he will oxidize or reduce it. The pieces of pottery resulting from these firings are called either pots—implying that oxidation is the usual way—or reduced pots, meaning those fired under reducing conditions.

That these terms refer to the manner of firing a kiln as well as the type of pottery coming from their firing implies that the appearance of pottery can be controlled by the manner of handling the firing. This is true, and has been known many centuries by potters, although at first it happened because of the circumstances of the firing and without the potter's understanding. As the centuries have passed, experience and knowledge have been handed down until now we know a vast amount about it.

Pottery is fired in conditions varying from oxidizing, through neutral, to strongly reducing. Manipulation of the fuel, air, and draft is involved in firing with or without a kiln. (Reducing in an electric kiln is a different matter, outside the scope of this discussion.) When air, over and above that necessary to burn the fuel, enters the kiln and surrounds the pots it is an oxidation firing; where only enough air is present to completely burn the fuel it is a neutral firing; where a scarcity of air, or an excess of fuel, prevails, an atmosphere is created that makes a reducing firing. Any time a damper is closed in a kiln the change will be in the direction of a reducing atmosphere. These varied conditions are more precisely controlled in a kiln than they are in an open fire.

But even without a kiln it is not too difficult to oxidize completely or reduce completely the ware in a controlled manner and with predictable results. Conditions in between these extremes are chancy, although the appearance of pottery so fired can be quite handsome. Interestingly enough, when firing is of the primitive kind, reduction is far easier to achieve than oxidation—just the reverse of a typical studio situation.

Steps showing pottery being buried at end of firing for reduced color, and cooled pots being dug out by Betty Feves several hours later.

When the potter is planning an oxidizing firing, his first thought must be how to get more than enough air to contact the pots during and after firing. The ways of controlling this are in the physical setting and in what is done at the conclusion of the firing.

A pottery setting raised somewhat above the ground and not in any shallow depression will bring pots up and into the air more. Several excellent color photographs in the February 1964 issue of *National Geographic* show this very type of setting as used by Mesa Verde potter Louisa Panana. The setting consists of a long, narrow iron trough supported on a number of tin cans; six or eight pots of a similar size and shape are in the trough, and the firing is done with long slats of wood placed tepee-fashion over the trough's length. As the wood burns and drops away sufficient air contacts the pots to ensure an oxidizing firing.

A pottery setting and firing as done by the Nigerians nowadays will seem to contradict both a condition necessary to oxidizing firing and my earlier warning of the dangers of cooling pots too fast. Their pots are not raised high above the ground and still they come from the fire an oxidized red brick color. The very large mass of pots like these retains heat a long time even though they are not buried. Slow cooling inhibits cracking and promotes oxidation.

The neutral, or "take-what-comes," firing, as I describe it, reflects an attitude that accepts whatever the firing does to the pot's color. It matters little how the pots are fired or what is done after the firing, in terms of oxidation and reduction, because one is not aiming for any specific results.

Two or three hours after reduction, pots are taken from sawdust and dirt.

A typical firing of this kind is as follows: Pots are set upon a piece of metal the usual five to six inches above the ground, or placed on a bed of twigs over a bed of hot coals; wood or dung is placed over the pottery, and the fire allowed to burn and reach maximum heat. The entire fire is buried and allowed to cool several hours. This handling of the firing produces pots with mottled patterns in colors of rust red, ochre, gray, and black with all of the subtle in-between variations. All of these colors do not appear on a white-burning clay, but only on clays containing iron oxide. During cooling and the continued smoldering of buried fuel, cover soil settles and exposes portions of the pots. When this happens, and where air reaches the pots, the color will be rust red; where less air contacts the pots the color will be gray; and where partly burned fuel touches them a black spot will remain. Occasionally an ochre color appears that must be the result of some condition not usually encountered. I have not yet been able to get an ochre color intentionally.

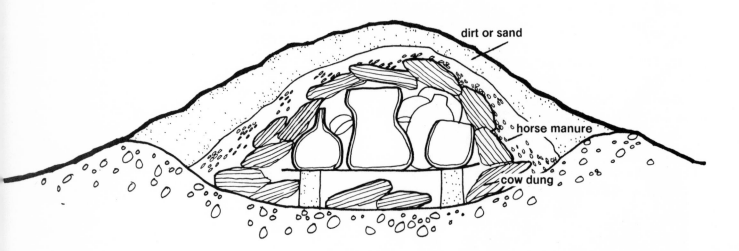

Cross-section of a reduction firing after being buried under manure and dirt.

Pots fired this way can be extremely handsome. When such a firing is planned the pots should be simple, strong in form, and devoid of complex decoration, because the fire will create its own chance decoration. Otherwise there will be a confusion on the pot's surface and neither a structural or applied texture nor the fire-created pattern have a chance to show with vigor.

Reducing pots in a primitive firing to obtain a total black is the easiest of the firings, I believe. Total and strong reduction must occur when the pots are in the most receptive condition. At the peak of firing a finely divided, dry fuel is shaken over the fire to smother it (powdered horse manure is excellent), while this in turn is completely and thoroughly buried under dry dirt. The operation must be done quickly, within two or three minutes. If pots have been protected with pieces of metal these should be removed with sticks after the burying. Cow or other animal dung, sawdust, and possibly rubber shavings can be used for the reduction. Pots are at their hottest at the end of firing and will hold their heat for a long time. Fresh fuel contacting the pots tries to burn, but since everything is buried no air can reach it and the result is a strong reducing atmosphere surrounding all the pottery. The entire mass of pots, dung, and dirt must be allowed to cool completely if the reduced black color is to be retained.

Change in the form of iron oxide in the clay, plus carbon particles absorbed into its surface pores, account for the black color. Surface carbon can be rubbed off.

All of the various colors resulting from different firing techniques are more intense on polished clay surfaces.

10.

Porosity

The methods of firing outlined in this book will not, in most instances, produce pottery that is watertight. Potters around the world who have worked with the primitive techniques that produced porous ware had ways of making their pots more or less watertight. We, who are not informed or practiced in their ways, believe glazes to be the only thing that makes a piece of pottery hold water. This is not always true by any means: unless the body of the pot is itself watertight and/or unless the glaze fits the pot without crazing or cracking, a glazed piece will leak.

Many people have asked me about using glazes when doing a pit or dung firing, and the answer is that it can be done. But will the results be acceptable? When glaze is being fired it becomes a molten liquid, and when it cools it becomes a hard glass. Wood or other fuel and ashes contact the pot while it is being fired, meaning that glazes may have ash and dirt imbedded in them when the firing is completed. Glaze might be used more properly on the insides of pots that are to be fired upside down, in which case the glaze would be protected from any contamination.

Reduced, polished pot. Double lobed red-ware bottle from Mosta-gedda, Middle Egypt, Predynastic (Negadi I) Period. (Photo, courtesy of the Trustees of the British Museum)

92

However, glaze requires far more precise firing than does clay. We are working with a very primitive technique, and pyrometric cones are not used to indicate heat. Therefore glazes in the usual sense are impractical and out of place.

The everyday living needs of primitive people are still simple, and the useful vessels they make are for storing grain or water, cooking their stews and mush, and for eating these foods. Cooking is often done over an open fire that does not damage or crack their low-fired pottery.

To make vessels watertight the Fiji Island potters swab pitch on the pieces as they are taken from the firing and are still hot, as an earlier illustration (page 83) shows.

Some of the southwest American Indians smeared a liquor on their pots, made by boiling desert plants or mesquite sap with water; it soaked into the clay pores and made a watertight vessel.

Regular use of a low-fired unglazed pot for cooking will, within a short time, render it watertight. One need not shudder at thinking this unsanitary. I have several such pots in constant use for cooking and baking, and they have a pleasant aroma to them.

In certain parts of the world porosity is a desirable feature of pottery. Slow seepage kept water cool in the water storage vessels used by peoples of the dry, southwest parts of the United States and other semi-arid areas.

Potters electing to work with the techniques described in this book should be fully aware of the historical backgrounds of these people, including their living habits, the climates they lived in, and the foods they ate. Our lives today are not the same and we therefore do not ordinarily have need for the kinds of pots they made. Some we can well use, while others will not fit our mode of life. It is a different matter if we are not thinking of useful pots, but are talking about sculptures or decorative and religious ceramic art.

11.

Traditional grate kiln with air vents at bottom, made of mud. Broken, fired shards inside support pottery. Men's pottery, Garki, Kano Province, Nigeria. (Photo by Jack Leggett)

Rudimentary Kilns

When tires form a temporary structure, or protecting wall, around pottery during firing, they represent an intermediate step in the evolution of firing, from no structure at all to the varied types of kilns used today. From this tire kiln that burns out and disappears, it is a short step to the primitive mud and clay walls built as a more or less permanent enclosure in which pottery is fired. The most permanent structure is built of bricks, or from a mixture high in clay content.

Although this kiln, if it can truthfully be called a kiln, finds its origin in antiquity, it is still used today. Nigerians at Garki, near Kano, turn out beautiful hand-made water flagons fired in a kiln like this. The accompanying illustration shows pots being unloaded from this kiln. This particular pottery happens to be a men's pottery (more often it is the women who are potters).

Famed Donna Rosa in Oaxaca, Mexico is a living potter who uses a kiln of this design. Hers is an enclosure dug as a pit below the ground's surface that has only a few openings at its base through which flames reach its interior. This suggests that kilns can be dug into the earth. It would be an advantage to do this on a sloping bank where the firebox mouth(s) would be at ground level.

Whether the kiln is built on or in the ground, and whether the size and details of construction vary, the concept is similar: a more or less permanent structure to fire pottery, providing a simple combustion chamber and allowing heat-carrying flames to surround the pottery.

In my own experience, using a wet clay mixture instead of bricks was first tried in the summer of 1970 during several workshops I held. Previous experiences with making firebox arches this way and firing them immediately convinced us that our workshop time limit of five days was no drawback to making an entire small kiln. In practice this was substantiated.

Fired, polished water flagons being taken from kiln after firing. (Men's pottery, Garki, Kano Province, Nigeria. (Photo by Jack Leggett)

We were uncertain if the kiln could be successfully fired wet, because we had been so completely trained to believe that only dry clay could be fired safely. We watched the kiln drying from a fire inside it and realized as it was steaming away that the fire was heating only the inside surface and therefore water was free to move outward and evaporate from the outside of the kiln. This first attempt to use wet clay in place of bricks was successful; others would follow. A series of photographs shows the construction and firing of a small kiln patterned after those of Nigerian design.

It can be assumed that the inside structure of the Nigerian kilns includes crisscrossing arched walls of clay that support the pottery and are high enough to allow good combustion underneath. Sometimes an even more primitive design was used, where the bottom of the kiln was filled with large, broken shards from previous firings.

The mixture to use in building such a kiln should consist of whatever clay is locally available and a fair amount of sand or some other inert mineral filler. A safe proportion is half and half, with the specific nature of the materials possibly indicating a different proportion. Lack of sufficient filler will cause the kiln structure to crack excessively while more than enough will form a weak structure.

Steps showing construction of a rudimentary kiln made of clay, sand, and sawdust. Scrap iron bars supported pottery above combustion area.

The kiln illustrated was built on the ground, with no preparation other than leveling an area big enough for it. When the kiln was about two-thirds built, two arched holes were cut into the walls opposite each other at ground level. Two small fireboxes were built and attached here. They were supported by scrap sheet aluminum bent to shape and left in place. Heat from the firing later melted away the aluminum.

Experience in building kilns out of clay rather than bricks shows that cracks in the walls can be expected wherever the form makes a right angle, such as where fireboxes join the kiln proper. These can, however, be patched. (A kiln built since this one has demonstrated an interesting fact: cracks develop only where there are angles to the kiln structure.)

The most effective drying of the kiln is done when it is empty, before any pots are put into it. The entire kiln must be completely dry before any real firing temperatures can be reached. With constant attention this can usually be done in half a day.

To those of us accustomed to stacking modern kilns with sillimanite or carborundum shelves, these kilns must indeed seem primitive, if not slipshod. But on careful inspection it will be seen that pots in these kilns are well supported on three or more points, a far better support than the one contact point they have on a kiln shelf.

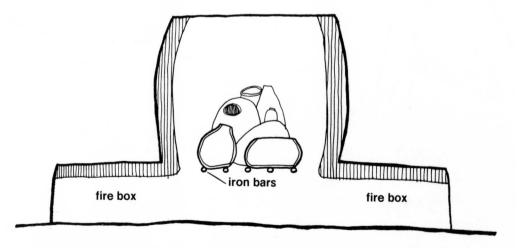

Cross-section of the rudimentary clay-sand kiln used for bisque and glaze firing.

The clay-sand kiln.

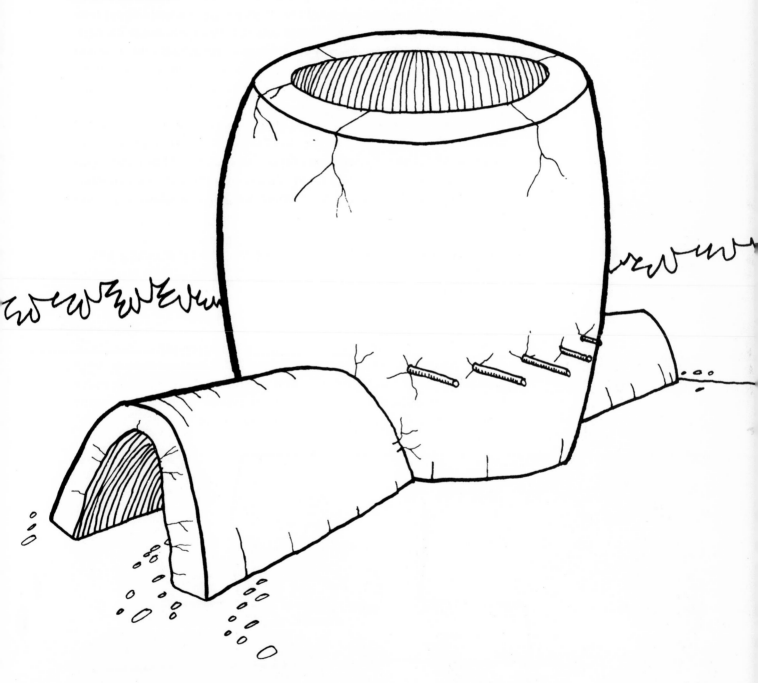

The Nigerians cover the kiln load of green, unfired pots with a layer of old tired shards for the purpose of retaining heat and making the temperatures more even. The same purpose is served in our kiln by partly covering the top with sheet metal. An even better way would be to narrow the kiln's top opening.

Firings in our kiln reached about 1,600° F. to 1,700° F., or approximately in the cone 010 to 08 range, and took about four hours.

These kilns are also appropriate for firing simple glazes on pots. Direct contact with fuel and ash is avoided, although smoke and flames do impinge upon the ware. Stacking glazed pieces demands the same judgment needed in stacking a studio kiln. An advantage over the studio kiln is the opportunity to look directly at the pots anytime during the firing to see how glaze fusion is progressing. In this sense it is similar to a raku firing.

Firing pottery in the clay kiln.

Metal partly covering kiln top helps keep heat inside.

Pouring sawdust into the kiln at peak of firing to reduce pottery.

12.

Kiln #6

More Sophisticated Kilns

Pit, or open, firing was followed by the development of kilns as a natural improvement over what was, at best, a very inefficient way to fire pottery. It is worth thinking about what makes a kiln better and what are the elements to incorporate in a kiln structure that will indeed make it an improvement.

The kilns described and illustrated in this chapter demonstrate mental flexibility on the part of the people who built them, and a willingness to adapt to the realities of their surroundings. The kilns appear to be very crude but at the same time they represent advances in design toward more efficient use of fuel, control over temperature, and the conservation of heat. They had to be adapted to geographical features of the areas where they were built and had to be made with whatever materials man discarded or nature provided.

There are certain theories about the construction of kilns that must be put into practice to the extent surrounding limitations allow. The theories may prove correct, or they may not, and when building a kiln it must be remembered that changes may have to be made.

A few simple rules about kilns will go a long way toward making them operate successfully.

The kiln is a tool for accumulating and using heat effectively; this is its primary function. Therefore anything having to do with fuel, air, and efficient combustion has to be considered carefully.

Draft—or the flow of air, heat, and gases—is basic to any kiln using fuel as a source of heat. Inadequate draft will mean less efficient combustion because not enough air will be drawn into the fire. Too vigorous a draft will draw excess air into the kiln, cooling it and carrying much of the heat out of the chimney. Draft is affected by various elements of kiln design. It is also the basis of designating two types of kilns, the down-draft and the updraft. A down-draft kiln is designed to make use of the working part of a flame where it is moving in a downward direction, while the up-draft kiln is heated by flames moving in an upward direction only.

Finding junk to help in building kilns.

Satisfactory rules of thumb have been handed down to us through the years which say that for each 3 feet of horizontal flame travel in the kiln, the chimney should be 1 foot high, and for every 1 foot of downward vertical flame travel the chimney should be 3 feet in height. Another rule applies to three different parts of the kiln through which air or flames and gases pass. They are designated as the firebox opening, where the primary air of combustion enters the kiln; the throat, or the opening(s) through which flames move from the firebox into the kiln chamber; and the flue or chimney, where flames and gases leave the kiln. According to the rule, the cross-sectional area of these three places should be similar. It is necessary that the firebox opening be adjustable to accommodate varying amounts of primary air for increasing amounts of fuel. It must also be possible to adjust the size of the flue opening in order to control the escape of gases from the kiln. For a neutral, ordinary firing only enough air to burn fuel completely should enter at the firebox mouth; more or less than this will cool the kiln. When either a reducing or oxidizing fire is wanted this rule is not followed; the potter ignores it in full knowledge of how to operate his kiln.

The relative sizes of the firebox and kiln chamber are not a constant proportion. When the kiln chamber is small, the firebox will be nearly equal in size. When the kiln chamber is larger, the firebox will be smaller in relation to it. For example, if the kiln is fired with wood and its chamber capacity is about 2 cubic feet, the firebox must be about equal in size. However, if the kiln chamber is 10 feet in capacity the firebox might have a capacity of only 4 cubic feet. As far as I know, there is no specific set of proportions to follow without resorting to highly technical and involved data outside the scope of this book. The potter must work by trial and error, and be guided by the elementary principles just set forth. Those principles were applied in making the six kilns described here.

Kiln # 1

My first experience with making kilns on a primitive level came during a pottery workshop near Death Valley in California. There were no bricks or ordinary kiln building materials at hand, nor was there even a dump that could supply inventive people with materials. An area a foot thick above the canyon floor was made and the kiln chamber built upon this. The kiln was up-draft in design and made from chunks of claylike earth. In front of, and lower than, the kiln chamber a firebox was added. The chimney was formed by blocking the face of a rain-cut channel in the canyon wall; it measured 8 feet in length and 8-by-8 inches in cross-section. Both the kiln chamber and firebox were approximately 2 cubic feet in capacity.

Fuel consisted of scrap wood and, for the first time in our experience, scraps of inner tubes and tires. No cones were used, and we knew nothing about the clay from which our pots were made. A good red heat was reached in four to five hours, a temperature sufficient in spots to melt a few pots. The kiln seemed to work well and was easy to stoke, although somewhat inconvenient to stack since the firebox had to be dismantled each time.

The Kiln is shown in operation on page 79.

Kiln # 2

An improved version of this kiln was made several years later at a near-by location. The same clayey earth was used in addition to some fire-brick, several sections of metal ventilating ducts, and various pieces of old sheet metal found nearby.

Cacti and tiny desert plants were the only vegetation around, but our work site was near what had once been a dumping ground for hundreds of old tires, so our fuel supply was guaranteed if we could find a good way to use tires!

It is nearly impossible to cut tires into small pieces, so the only solution was to burn them whole, one at a time. This required some thinking and planning.

Definite limitations were imposed by the materials at hand, so it was decided that the tires must be placed into a firebox vertically and burned that way; the firebox could be narrow and a roof easily made to span it. The other major concern was the widely varying heat entering the kiln when burning tires one at a time, at intervals. Therefore the entire kiln was elongated and its separate parts made long and narrow, much like the vital organs of a snake. This had a softening, evening effect on heat entering the kiln chamber.

The distance from firebox mouth to chimney top was about 20 feet, while the size of the kiln chamber proper was 5 feet long and about 18 inches square. Photographs show the tall, narrow firebox cut into a bank, the 6-foot-long throat, the kiln chamber, and a section of flue pipe in place that was removed for stacking and unstacking the kiln.

Steps in building and firing kiln #2.
Note elongated kiln chamber
and narrow firebox.

Steps in building and firing kiln #3. Note almost horizontal position of kiln.

Kiln # 3

Another similar kiln was built and is illustrated here. It differed mainly in that the kiln chamber roof was opened for access, the total length of the kiln was over 30 feet, and the chimney was more horizontal than vertical.

When rubber tires burn they disintegrate into particles similar in size to those of sawdust. Like a pile of burning sawdust, the rubber must be stirred frequently to burn hot and completely. The tire's beads (coils of wire) also litter the fire and should be removed.

The heat distribution in these kilns was not even, but there was remarkably little variation under the circumstances. Many good pieces came from several firings, along with a few that melted. The firings took about six hours to finish. Temperature was estimated to be between cone 2 and cone 6. One fine piece, glazed with a desert alkali, is illustrated.

Tire-burning up-draft kiln of clayey earth blocks.

Fired pot of desert clay mixed with some desert alkali. From kiln #3.

Fired pot glazed with desert alkali. From kiln #3.

Kiln # 4

Bricking up door of salt-glazing kiln.

Firebox built back into place, and fire started in salt-glazing kiln.

A salt-glazing kiln was the largest ever attempted by students at any of my workshops. It was a round, down-draft kiln dug into a river bank of clay and silt; its construction required few man-made materials. Measuring 5 feet in height and 5 feet in diameter, it had a chimney running from the rear floor, up through a bank, and extending vertically another 10 feet. Standard flue tile formed the last part of the chimney, the total length of which was about 20 feet. The opening of the kiln chamber was arched with fire-brick and the firebox built in place against it for each firing. The firebox measured 5 feet long, 2 feet wide, and 3 feet high; these dimensions included an ash pit under a grate of heavy iron bars. Pots in the front of the kiln were protected by a flame-deflecting brick (bag) wall just inside the kiln opening, which also directed flames upward into the kiln dome.

Wood left from spring flooding of the stream was cut into proper lengths for the firebox and used to fire the kiln. It took from eleven to thirteen hours to reach cone 6. Higher temperatures were not attempted. At cone 6 the kiln ceiling started to melt, slough off, and fall onto the ware. Pots firing in the kiln were also made from this river bank silt and could not stand any higher temperatures. As it was, a few molten bits of silt, looking like three-dimensional *temmoku* glaze, fell from the roof of the kiln and stuck to several pots.

Salting followed the normal procedure of introducing a wetted mixture of rock salt and borax into the kiln at intervals beginning at cone 3 and continuing until the firing was completed. Draw tiles were also used to show the progress of salt-glaze formation. These are looped bits of clay drawn from the kiln through the spy hole with a long iron rod.

An evaluation of this experience indicated that an approach with novel, unpredictable results in making and firing pots would be worthwhile. Namely, flat forms could be intentionally made to catch droppings from the kiln ceiling; the kiln could be fired somewhat higher than cone 6, in which event any droppings would probably fuse to the firing pottery.

Checking temperature in salt-glaze firing. Cones are just barely visible at bottom of peephole.

Our experience with this salt-glaze kiln actually anticipated the use of sand and clay as a structural material, replacing bricks for building kilns.

Previously we had learned a wet clay kiln could be fired safely; we knew it would not blow up as long as one surface of the clay was open to the air. Would our success continue when part of the outside surface was not free to the air, but buried in dirt?

Kiln # 5

Only one kiln was attempted the first time this idea was tried out. It was dried and fired just as previous kilns were, without mishap. Five more such kilns were immediately built and all were successful. A few weeks later the construction of seven more kilns that were also successful proved that no problems would be encountered.

Although the inside surfaces of all these kilns became hard and permanent from the heat, the outside surfaces, including those buried in the earth, remained as unfired, dry clay. This made no difference, since the kilns were not going to be kept. If a person wanted a permanent kiln that would withstand the weather, he would have to fire the entire structure by building a huge fire over it.

Each kiln was made by a different group of people, so no two were alike. Their forms and the embellishments on them were fascinating; people were building pieces of sculpture, although they hardly realized it. Teachers might take a tip from this as a way to free unconscious creative expression.

Kiln # 6

Kiln #6 with dome partly removed for stacking. Note finely split wood and chimney at one side.

At the Haystack School in Maine, two students made what was the most sophisticated kiln that could be described within the scope of this book. It was wood fired and, in terms of design and materials, was more traditional than any of the above kilns.

A round, dome-shaped kiln was built of common brick and firebrick. The top several layers of brick were removed for access to the firing chamber. The chimney consisted of flue pipe atop the dome; it too was removed and replaced each time the kiln was opened.

A false floor in the kiln chamber directed flames under and around the sides of the pottery. Regular kiln shelves and supports were used in stacking the ware. The firebox had no grate and was originally too small; it was later doubled in length for more satisfactory firing. Photographs show where this addition was made.

The original dimensions of the kiln were 3 feet in diameter and 3 feet high; the firebox was 2 feet wide by 1½ feet high; its original 2-foot length was later extended to 5 feet.

An experience like this points to what many studio potters are not aware of: compared to gas, wood is bulky and needs much more space in which to burn well. Most potters fire their kilns with gas and blowers that produce a hot flame and need little space in which to do it. The scale of a wood-burning firebox is outside their experience, and they seem consistently to build them too small. Therefore the kind of fuel used should be one of the first considerations influencing the designing of a kiln.

Wood is a marvellous fuel for firing pottery and helps produce effects not obtainable any other way. The Japanese are well aware of this. They are masters of firing with wood. When they start firing a kiln it is with slow-burning large logs and, as the kiln temperature increases, smaller and smaller pieces of wood are used until, at the end of the firing when the heat is greatest, finely split wood is used which almost explodes when thrown into the firebox or kiln.

Kiln #6 being fired with wood. Note how firebox has been extended in length.

Looking at cones inside kiln to check firing progress.

Wood is much slower in catching fire than gas, and the stoker should know this. The early stages of firing are more relaxed than are the later stages, when stoking has to be done every two or three minutes. This is a demanding job that cannot tolerate distractions. Invariably one or two people constantly attending a fire will develop the necessary rhythm of stoking that a continually changing personnel cannot achieve.

In summary, the following points concerning kiln design and fuel must be considered: available structural materials; available fuel; overall sizes of the kiln chamber and firebox; down-draft or up-draft function; access to kiln chamber; form and size of flue; control of combustion air; ease of stoking, and ash removal (if wood fired).

The kilns described and illustrated here were, in their physical aspects, somewhat crude. That they all fired successfully (some with adjustment) shows that the thought behind their design and construction was sound.

A final bit of advice to a potter attempting projects like these is that he be where he is. By this I mean that his mind and thinking, as well as his body, must be where he is working and not elsewhere. The reality of his situation is all around him and visible in his surroundings; it is not at his home or workshop. Knowledge and experience out of his past are helpful, if not essential, but he is not in the past. He is in and of today, where he is, at the moment. Then his mind will be open and receptive.

It is good to approach these experiences as explorations and discoveries. The potter will then be in a mood to plan his activities rationally, and to accept results that have previously been outside his experience.

References and Suggested Reading

Bjørn, Arne. *Exploring Fire and Clay.* New York: Van Nostrand Reinhold Company, 1969.

Christensen, Edwin O. *Primitive Art.* New York: Crown Publishers, 1955.

Fontana, Bernard L. et al. *Papago Indian Pottery.* Seattle: University of Washington Press, 1962.

La Farge, Oliver. *Pictorial History of the American Indian.* New York: Crown Publishers, 1959.

Shanklin, Margaret. *Use of Native Craft Materials.* Peoria, Illinois: Manual Arts Press, 1947.

Shepard, Anna O. *Ceramics for the Archaeologist.* Carnegie Institution of Washington (Publication #609), 1968.

Turner, Clara Lee. *Southwest Indian Craft Arts.* Tuscon: University of Arizona Press, 1968.

Underhill, Ruth. *Pueblo Crafts.* Washington: Bureau of Indian Affairs, U.S. Department of the Interior, 1944.

Index

Jacket:
Red heat of a firing pot visible through embers.

Back of jacket:
Author firing pottery with wood.